DALE MATTHEWS-NG

Unveiling Grand Rapids, Ohio

A Journey from Unfamiliarity to Appreciation

Contents

Introduction

Welcome to "Unveiling Grand Rapids, Ohio," a journey into the heart of a village where history and charm intertwine seamlessly. Whether you're a curious traveler, a history enthusiast, or someone seeking the warmth of small-town America, this book aims to transform your unfamiliarity into a deep appreciation for Grand Rapids, Ohio.

Nestled along the Maumee River, Grand Rapids is a village that beautifully preserves its past while embracing the present. Established in 1833 as Gilead, it was later renamed Grand Rapids in 1868, reflecting its connection to the river's rapids. The village's rich history is evident in its well-preserved architecture, with many buildings listed on the National Register of Historic Places.

As you turn these pages, you'll discover the unique charm that defines Grand Rapids. From the annual Applebutter Fest, which celebrates traditional crafts and local heritage, to the serene beauty of the Maumee River, the village offers a tapestry of experiences that captivate the heart.

This book is crafted to be both informative and engaging, inviting you to explore the stories, landmarks, and traditions that make Grand Rapids a hidden gem in Ohio. Through vivid narratives and historical insights, we hope to bring the village's legacy to life, offering you a window into its enduring spirit.

Join us as we unveil the essence of Grand Rapids, Ohio—a place where history lives on every corner, and the community's warmth welcomes all who visit.

Chapter 1: Early History and Founding

Native American Heritage

The Maumee River area has been home to various Native American tribes for thousands of years. Notable among these were the Miami, Ottawa (Odawa), Shawnee, and Wyandot tribes. Each tribe added to the rich culture of the region, setting up villages along the river and engaging in diverse social and economic activities.

Tribes of the Maumee River Region

- **Miami Tribe**: Originally from Indiana and southern Michigan, the Miami moved into the Maumee Valley around 1700, becoming one of the most powerful tribes in Ohio. They established villages along the river, utilizing its resources for sustenance and transportation.
- **Ottawa (Odawa) Tribe**: The Ottawa had a significant presence at the mouth of the Maumee River and occupied other territories in northwestern Ohio, including along its tributary, the Blanchard River. Their name for the Miami tribe, "Maamii," is the origin of the river's name.

- **Shawnee and Wyandot Tribes**: These tribes also inhabited the Maumee River region, contributing to the area's diverse Indigenous culture. They engaged in hunting, fishing, and agriculture, utilizing the river's resources for their livelihoods.

Culture, Trade, and Interactions with Early Settlers

The Maumee River was a crucial route for trade and communication among Native American tribes and later between them and European settlers. The river allowed the exchange of goods like furs, tools, and food, leading to economic interdependence. As European settlers arrived, they engaged in the profitable fur trade, influencing Native American culture by introducing trade goods such as silver, clothing, and weapons.

Interactions between Native Americans and settlers were complex, involving both cooperation and conflict. The Battle of Fallen Timbers in 1794, fought near the Maumee River, was a significant event where U.S. forces defeated a group of Native American tribes, leading to major land losses and changing the region's cultural landscape.

Archaeological Findings in the Maumee River Area

Archaeological studies have found artifacts from the Woodland Indian period (500 BC to 1100 AD) near the Maumee River and its floodplains. These findings include tools, pottery, and remains of homes, showing that Native Americans not only hunted and gathered along the riverbanks but also built homes and grew crops.

Excavations at sites like the Fry Site (33Lu165) have uncovered Ottawa farmsteads dating from A.D. 1814-1832, including structures such as cabins and animal pens, as well as a variety of Native and Euro-American artifacts.

These discoveries provide valuable insights into the daily lives, economic activities, and cultural practices of the Native Americans who lived in the Maumee River region.

Through these archaeological efforts, we gain a deeper understanding of the rich Native American heritage that continues to influence the Maumee River region today.

Settlement and Establishment

In the early 19th century, European settlers began moving into the Maumee River region, attracted by its fertile land and strategic location. Among the pioneers was Thomas Howard, a Revolutionary War veteran who, in 1812, traveled by boat across Lake Erie to the head of the rapids, becoming the first settler of what would later become Grand Rapids, Ohio. His family joined him after walking through the woods of Pennsylvania and Ohio. Other settlers soon followed, drawn by the promise of new opportunities in the area.

Founding of Gilead in 1833

The growing community led to the formal establishment of the town of Gilead in 1833. The village was platted that year, marking the official recognition of the settlement. The name "Gilead" was chosen, reflecting the settlers' aspirations for their new home.

Village Layout and Initial Infrastructure

The layout of Gilead was typical of early American frontier towns. The village was platted with a grid pattern, featuring two public squares that served as central gathering places for the community. These squares were integral to the village's social and economic life, hosting markets, public meetings, and other communal activities.

The initial infrastructure of Gilead included essential establishments such as general stores, blacksmith shops, and mills, which were vital for the settlers' daily needs and the village's economic development. The proximity to the Maumee River facilitated transportation and trade, further contributing to the village's growth.

In the 1840s, the state of Ohio built a large dam across the Maumee River at Gilead to support canal operations. However, this dam replaced a smaller one that had powered a local mill, leading to discontent among the villagers. In response, the citizens destroyed the new dam, prompting the construction of a side-cut canal that connected Gilead with the main canal. This development spurred an economic boom in the village.

The establishment of Gilead in 1833 marked the beginning of a vibrant community that would continue to grow and evolve, laying the foundation for the village known today as Grand Rapids, Ohio.

Impact of the Miami and Erie Canal

The Miami and Erie Canal, stretching approximately 274 miles from Cincinnati to Toledo, Ohio, was a monumental infrastructure project of the 19th century. Construction commenced in 1825 and concluded in 1845, with the canal serving as a vital link between the Ohio River and Lake Erie. Its primary purpose was to facilitate the efficient movement of goods and people across the state, thereby enhancing trade and fostering economic growth.

Boosting Local Commerce and Transportation

The canal significantly reduced transportation costs and time, making it more economical to move agricultural products, raw materials, and manufactured goods. This efficiency led to a surge in local commerce, as businesses could now access broader markets. Towns along the canal's route, including Grand Rapids, Ohio, experienced increased trade activity, with merchants and farmers benefiting from the improved transportation network.

Influence on Population Growth and Economic Development

The enhanced transportation infrastructure attracted settlers, leading to population growth in canal-adjacent communities. The availability of reliable transportation encouraged the establishment of new businesses and industries, contributing to the economic development of the region. The canal's presence transformed previously isolated areas into thriving hubs of activity, laying the groundwork for future prosperity.

In summary, the Miami and Erie Canal played a pivotal role in shaping the economic landscape of Ohio. Its construction facilitated commerce, improved transportation, and spurred population growth, leaving a lasting legacy on the communities it connected.

Chapter 2: Evolution Through the 19th and 20th Centuries

Industrial Growth

In the mid-19th century, Grand Rapids, Ohio, experienced significant industrial development, primarily driven by its strategic location along the Maumee River and the establishment of the Miami and Erie Canal. These factors facilitated the emergence of key industries, notably milling and agriculture, which became the backbone of the village's economy.

Key Industries: Milling and Agriculture

The abundant water resources of the Maumee River provided the necessary power for milling operations. Numerous mills were established along the riverbanks, processing grains and other agricultural products from the surrounding fertile lands. This milling industry not only supplied local needs but also catered to markets beyond the village, thanks to the efficient transportation routes offered by the canal. Agriculture thrived alongside milling, with farmers cultivating crops that supported both local consumption and trade.

Establishment of the First Dam and Its Significance

To harness the river's power more effectively, the first dam was constructed in the late 1830s. This dam played a crucial role in regulating water flow, ensuring a consistent and reliable source of energy for the mills. The controlled water levels facilitated year-round milling operations, significantly boosting production capacity and economic stability. The dam's construction marked a pivotal moment in the village's industrialization, laying the foundation for sustained growth and prosperity.

Notable Businesses and Entrepreneurs of the Era

Several enterprising individuals and businesses emerged during this period, contributing to the village's economic landscape. One prominent figure was Benjamin F. Kerr, who succeeded previous proprietors in operating a longstanding business enterprise in the village. Born in Richland County, Ohio, in 1843, Kerr moved to Lucas County in 1848 and later became a key player in the local business community. His leadership and entrepreneurial spirit exemplified the dynamic economic environment of Grand Rapids during this era.

Another notable entrepreneur was Frank M. Stump, who, along with his brothers, emigrated from Germany and operated Crystal Mills in Grand Rapids around 1890. The Stump family's milling operations contributed significantly to the local economy, demonstrating the vital role of immigrant entrepreneurs in the village's industrial growth.

These industries and individuals collectively propelled Grand

Rapids into a period of economic prosperity, establishing a legacy of industrial growth that would influence the village's development for decades to come.

Transportation Advancements

In 1877, Grand Rapids, Ohio, experienced a significant transformation with the arrival of the railroad. This development marked a pivotal shift in the village's transportation infrastructure, influencing local commerce and daily life.

Arrival of the Railroad in 1877

The introduction of the railroad in 1877 provided Grand Rapids with a more efficient and reliable means of transportation. Unlike the canal, which was susceptible to seasonal limitations such as freezing in winter, the railroad offered year-round service. This advancement facilitated faster movement of goods and passengers, enhancing connectivity with larger markets and contributing to the village's economic growth.

Comparing the Railroad's Impact to the Canal

While the Miami and Erie Canal had been instrumental in the village's early development, the railroad introduced several advantages:

- Speed and Efficiency: Trains could transport goods and passengers much faster than canal boats, reducing travel time significantly.
- Year-Round Operation: The railroad operated regardless

of weather conditions, unlike the canal, which was often closed during winter months due to freezing.

- Expanded Reach: Rail networks connected Grand Rapids to a broader range of destinations, facilitating more extensive trade opportunities.

These factors collectively made the railroad a more attractive option for transportation and commerce.

Decline of Canal Usage with the Rise of Rail Transport

The emergence of the railroad led to a gradual decline in canal usage. Businesses and travelers favored the speed and reliability of trains over the slower canal boats. Additionally, the maintenance costs of the canal became increasingly burdensome, leading to its eventual abandonment. By the early 20th century, the canal had largely ceased operations, marking the end of an era in Grand Rapids' transportation history.

In summary, the arrival of the railroad in 1877 marked a significant advancement in Grand Rapids' transportation landscape, offering superior speed, efficiency, and connectivity compared to the canal. This shift not only enhanced local commerce but also signaled the decline of canal transportation in favor of rail, shaping the village's economic trajectory in the years that followed.

Community Development

The late 19th century was a transformative period for Grand Rapids, Ohio, marked by the establishment of essential institutions and the community's resilience in the face of adversity.

Establishment of Schools, Churches, and Civic Organizations

As Grand Rapids grew, the community prioritized education, faith, and civic engagement. Schools were established to provide education to the village's youth, laying the foundation for future generations. Churches became central to community life, offering spiritual guidance and serving as gathering places for residents. Civic organizations also emerged, fostering community spirit and addressing local needs. These institutions collectively contributed to the village's social fabric and development.

Devastating Fires of the Late 1890s

In the late 1890s, Grand Rapids faced significant challenges due to a series of devastating fires. These fires ravaged the village, destroying homes, businesses, and public buildings. The destruction was extensive, impacting the community's economy and displacing many residents. Despite these hardships, the community's spirit remained unbroken.

Resilience and Rebuilding Efforts

In the aftermath of the fires, the residents of Grand Rapids demonstrated remarkable resilience. They undertook rebuilding efforts with determination, reconstructing homes and businesses and restoring the village's infrastructure. This period of reconstruction not only rebuilt physical structures but also strengthened community bonds. The collective effort to restore the village showcased the community's unwavering spirit and commitment to their home.

Through the establishment of key institutions and the community's response to adversity, Grand Rapids, Ohio, exemplified resilience and unity, laying a strong foundation for its future development.

Chapter 3: Preservation and Modern Identity

Architectural Heritage

Grand Rapids, Ohio, boasts a rich architectural heritage, characterized by its Victorian-era structures and dedicated preservation efforts.

Victorian Architecture in the Village

The village's architectural landscape is dominated by Victorian-style buildings, featuring ornate brickwork, elaborate moldings, and decorative transom windows. These design elements reflect the aesthetic preferences of the late 19th century, showcasing the craftsmanship and artistic sensibilities of that era. The downtown shopping district serves as a prime example, where restored canal buildings exhibit these distinctive Victorian features.

Restoration Efforts Initiated in 1975

In 1975, a concerted effort to restore and preserve the village's Victorian architecture began, aiming to revitalize Grand Rapids while honoring its historical character. This initiative focused on rehabilitating aging structures, ensuring their structural integrity, and maintaining their original design elements. The restoration not only enhanced the village's aesthetic appeal but also reinforced its historical identity, attracting visitors and fostering community pride.

Buildings Listed on the National Register of Historic Places

Several notable buildings in Grand Rapids are recognized on the National Register of Historic Places, underscoring their historical and architectural significance:

- **Grand Rapids Town Hall**: Constructed in 1898 in the Romanesque style, this building has served as a central hub for municipal activities and stands as a testament to the village's civic heritage.
- **Thurston Building**: Erected in 1896, this structure has housed various businesses over the years, including a pharmacy operated by multiple owners. Its enduring presence highlights the village's commercial history.
- **Kerr House**: Located at 17605 Beaver Street, this building contributes to the village's historical narrative, reflecting the architectural styles and community developments of its time.

These buildings not only exemplify the architectural heritage of Grand Rapids but also serve as tangible links to its past, enriching the village's cultural landscape.

Through dedicated restoration efforts and the preservation of its Victorian architecture, Grand Rapids, Ohio, continues to celebrate and maintain its historical legacy, offering residents and visitors alike a glimpse into its storied past.

Cultural Events and Traditions

Grand Rapids, Ohio, is a village rich in cultural events and traditions that foster community spirit and celebrate its heritage.

The Annual Applebutter Fest and Its Origins

Since 1977, the Applebutter Fest has been a cherished tradition in Grand Rapids, drawing over 30,000 attendees each year. Organized by the Historical Society of Grand Rapids, Ohio, the festival began as a modest gathering aimed at demonstrating pioneer and farm-life skills. It has since evolved into a vibrant event featuring historical reenactments, artisan crafts, live music, and, of course, the preparation and sale of apple butter—a nod to the region's agricultural roots.

Other Local Festivals and Community Gatherings

Beyond the Applebutter Fest, Grand Rapids hosts various events that strengthen community bonds:

- **Rhythm on the River Arts Series**: Sponsored by the Historical Society, this series brings musical performances to the Wright Pavilion, offering residents and visitors an opportunity to enjoy live entertainment in a scenic setting.

- **Annual Dinner and Silent Auction**: This event combines fine dining with fundraising, featuring a silent auction and entertainment to support local initiatives.
- **Grand Rapids Bloodmobiles**: Regular blood drives are held at Hosanna Lutheran Church, encouraging community participation in life-saving efforts.

These gatherings play a crucial role in maintaining the village's close-knit atmosphere and fostering civic engagement.

The Role of the Historical Society in Preserving Traditions

The Historical Society of Grand Rapids, Ohio, established in 1975, is dedicated to educating the public about the region's rich history and bringing the community together through cultural events. The Society organizes the Applebutter Fest and other activities, ensuring that the village's traditions are celebrated and passed down through generations. Additionally, the Society supports other local nonprofits, further contributing to the community's cultural preservation.

Through these events and the efforts of the Historical Society, Grand Rapids continues to honor its heritage while fostering a vibrant and engaged community.

Tourism and Recreation

Grand Rapids, Ohio, offers a blend of historical attractions, outdoor activities, and local businesses that cater to visitors seeking a unique and enriching experience.

Isaac Ludwig Mill and Canal Boat Rides

A centerpiece of Grand Rapids' historical charm is the Isaac Ludwig Mill, located within Providence Metropark. This working water-powered saw and gristmill provides visitors with a glimpse into 19th-century milling operations. Adjacent to the mill, the canal boat "The Volunteer," a reproduction of a mule-drawn canal boat, offers rides along a restored section of the Miami and Erie Canal. These rides allow guests to experience the transportation methods of the past, complete with passage through an original lock.

Outdoor Activities in Providence Metropark

Providence Metropark is a haven for outdoor enthusiasts. The park features more than a mile of the original Miami and Erie Canal and towpath, providing scenic trails for hiking and biking. The Providence Dam, constructed across the Maumee River, offers picturesque views and fishing opportunities. Additionally, the park includes picnic facilities, a playground, and access points for kayaking on the Maumee River Water Trail.

Local Businesses Catering to Visitors

The village's historic downtown is lined with businesses that enhance the visitor experience:

- **Antique Shops**: Establishments like Antiques on Front offer a curated selection of vintage items, including antique lighting, furniture, and art.
- **Eateries**: Local restaurants provide a variety of dining options, from casual cafes to fine dining, ensuring that visitors can enjoy meals that suit their preferences.

These businesses, along with the village's historical and natural attractions, make Grand Rapids a compelling destination for tourists seeking a blend of history, recreation, and local charm.

Chapter 4: Looking Ahead – Future Prospects

Economic Development in Grand Rapids, Ohio

Grand Rapids, Ohio, is a village that harmoniously blends its rich historical heritage with contemporary economic initiatives, fostering a vibrant community for both residents and businesses.

Current Economic Drivers and Employment Opportunities

The local economy thrives on a mix of small businesses, tourism, and light industry. The historic downtown area is home to various shops, restaurants, and service providers, contributing significantly to the village's economic vitality. Tourism, bolstered by attractions like the Isaac Ludwig Mill and the annual Applebutter Fest, plays a crucial role in supporting local enterprises. Additionally, light industrial operations, such as Buckeye Hydraulics and D. Jones Tool & Die, offer employment opportunities and contribute to the economic landscape.

Initiatives to Attract New Businesses and Residents

To stimulate economic growth, Grand Rapids has designated over 40 acres of land for development, aiming to attract new businesses and residents. The Grand Rapids Area Chamber of Commerce actively promotes local enterprises and organizes events to enhance community engagement and visibility. Collaborations with regional economic development organizations, like the Wood County Economic Development Commission, provide resources and support for prospective businesses considering relocation or expansion into the area.

Balancing Growth with Preserving Small-Town Charm

As Grand Rapids pursues economic development, maintaining its small-town charm remains a priority. Efforts are made to ensure that new developments align with the village's historical character and community values. The preservation of historic sites and the organization of traditional events, such as the Applebutter Fest, reflect the community's commitment to honoring its heritage while embracing growth. This careful balance fosters a unique environment where economic progress coexists with the preservation of the village's distinctive identity.

Through strategic initiatives and a dedication to its cultural roots, Grand Rapids continues to evolve as a dynamic community that offers economic opportunities while retaining the qualities that make it a cherished place to live and visit.

Community Engagement in Grand Rapids, Ohio

Grand Rapids, Ohio, is a village distinguished by its active community organizations, dedicated volunteers, and educational programs that celebrate and preserve its rich history and culture.

Active Community Organizations and Their Roles

Several organizations play pivotal roles in fostering community spirit and cultural preservation:

- **Historical Society of Grand Rapids Ohio**: Established in 1975, the society is committed to educating the public about the region's history. It organizes events like the annual Applebutter Fest and "Rhythm on the River" concerts, and maintains historical sites such as the Welcome Log Cabin and Lincoln Street. The society also supports other local organizations and educational programs within the community.
- **Grand Rapids Arts Council**: This council promotes the arts through various events and programs, enriching the cultural fabric of the village.
- **Grand Rapids Chamber of Commerce**: The chamber supports local businesses and organizes community events, contributing to the village's economic vitality and communal cohesion.

Volunteerism and Civic Participation

Volunteerism is integral to Grand Rapids' community life. Residents actively participate in organizing and supporting events like the Applebutter Fest, which serves as a significant fundraiser for local organizations. The Historical Society, for instance, relies on volunteers for event planning, maintenance of historical sites, and educational outreach. This collective effort not only strengthens community bonds but also ensures the sustainability of local traditions and initiatives.

Educational Programs Promoting Local History and Culture

Educational initiatives are central to promoting and preserving the village's heritage:

- **School Programs**: The Historical Society collaborates with Otsego Local Schools to provide educational programs that immerse students in the local history and cultural practices of Grand Rapids.
- **Community Events**: Events such as the Applebutter Fest and "Rhythm on the River" concerts serve as platforms for cultural education, offering residents and visitors alike opportunities to engage with the village's traditions and historical narratives.

Through the concerted efforts of its community organizations, dedicated volunteers, and comprehensive educational programs, Grand Rapids, Ohio, continues to foster a vibrant and engaged community that honors its rich heritage while embracing the future.

Sustainability and Preservation in Grand Rapids, Ohio

Grand Rapids, Ohio, is dedicated to preserving its historical sites and natural resources while embracing sustainable practices for future development.

Maintaining Historical Sites and Natural Resources

The village has undertaken several initiatives to preserve its rich heritage:

- **Historical Society of Grand Rapids Ohio**: Founded in 1975, this organization focuses on educating the public about the region's history and organizing cultural events. It also supports other local nonprofits in their preservation efforts.
- **Restoration Projects**: Significant restoration efforts have been made, such as the revitalization of Lincoln Street in 2017, which included landscaping, a water feature, and a commemorative plaque honoring contributors to the village's transformation.

Environmental Initiatives

The community actively engages in environmental preservation:

- **FreshWater Accountability Project**: This initiative ad-

dresses environmental concerns in rural communities, including Grand Rapids, focusing on the exploitation of natural resources by polluting industries.
- **H2Ohio Chloride Reduction Grant**: The village received $54,925 to upgrade equipment and salt storage facilities, aiming to reduce environmental impact.

Future Infrastructure Improvements Honoring Heritage

Plans are in place to ensure that future developments respect the village's historical character:

- **National Register of Historic Places**: Grand Rapids has five buildings listed on the National Register, reflecting its commitment to preserving historical architecture.
- **Community Engagement**: Local organizations, such as the Grand Rapids Arts Council and the Chamber of Commerce, work together to promote sustainable development that aligns with the village's heritage.

Through these combined efforts, Grand Rapids, Ohio, continues to honor its past while fostering a sustainable and vibrant future.

Conclusion: Embracing the Timeless Charm of Grand Rapids, Ohio

As we conclude our journey through the rich tapestry of Grand Rapids, Ohio, it's evident why this village stands as a beacon of history, culture, and community spirit. Nestled along the Maumee River, Grand Rapids offers visitors a unique blend of historical significance and small-town charm.

Why Visit Grand Rapids, Ohio?

- **Historical Significance**: Established in the early 19th century, Grand Rapids has preserved its heritage through well-maintained Victorian architecture and landmarks like the Isaac Ludwig Mill. Visitors can step back in time with canal boat rides that echo the village's past.
- **Cultural Events**: The annual Applebutter Fest is a testament to the village's commitment to celebrating its traditions. This festival, among others, offers a glimpse into the community's vibrant cultural life.
- **Recreational Activities**: Providence Metropark provides ample opportunities for outdoor enthusiasts, from hiking trails to fishing spots, all set against the backdrop of the scenic Maumee River.

- **Local Businesses**: A stroll through the village reveals a variety of antique shops, boutiques, and eateries, each offering unique products and flavors that reflect the local character.

Our Exploration

Throughout this book, we've delved into the multifaceted history and culture of Grand Rapids:

- **Native American Heritage**: We explored the indigenous tribes that once inhabited the Maumee River region, their rich cultures, and their interactions with early settlers.
- **Settlement and Establishment**: The founding of Gilead in 1833 marked the beginning of a community that would evolve into the Grand Rapids we know today.
- **Impact of the Miami and Erie Canal**: The canal's construction was pivotal in boosting local commerce and transportation, leading to significant economic development.
- **Industrial Growth**: Industries such as milling and agriculture flourished, with the establishment of the first dam playing a crucial role in the village's growth.
- **Transportation Advancements**: The arrival of the railroad in 1877 marked a new era, gradually overshadowing canal usage and reshaping the village's transportation landscape.
- **Community Development**: Despite challenges like the devastating fires of the late 1890s, the community's resilience led to the establishment of schools, churches, and civic organizations.

- **Architectural Heritage**: The village's Victorian architecture has been meticulously preserved, with several buildings listed on the National Register of Historic Places.
- **Cultural Events and Traditions**: Festivals like the Applebutter Fest and the efforts of the Historical Society have been instrumental in preserving and celebrating local traditions.
- **Tourism and Recreation**: Attractions such as the Isaac Ludwig Mill, canal boat rides, and Providence Metropark offer visitors a blend of history and outdoor activities.
- **Economic Development**: Balancing growth with the preservation of small-town charm remains a priority, with initiatives aimed at attracting new businesses and residents.
- **Community Engagement**: Active community organizations, volunteerism, and educational programs play a vital role in fostering a strong sense of community.
- **Sustainability and Preservation**: Efforts to maintain historical sites, natural resources, and environmental initiatives underscore the village's commitment to a sustainable future.

In essence, Grand Rapids, Ohio, is more than just a destination; it's a living narrative of resilience, tradition, and community. Whether you're drawn by its history, cultural events, recreational opportunities, or the warmth of its residents, a visit to Grand Rapids promises an enriching experience that bridges the past with the present.

Thank you for accompanying us on this exploration of Grand Rapids, Ohio. Your interest in this village's story is greatly appreciated. If you found this book informative and engaging, please consider leaving a review on Amazon. Your feedback helps others discover the charm and history of Grand Rapids.

Resources

A brief history. (n.d.). HISTORICAL SOCIETY OF GRAND RAPIDS OHIO. https://www.grandrapidsh istoricalsociety.org/a-brief-history.html

About this Place: Once Home to 40 Tribes and the Traditional Home of the Shawnee Peoples | Ohio University. (n.d.). https://www.ohio.edu/cas/ping-institute/humanities-park/fir st-humanists/about-place

Alexandra Bevins - Defiance College. (2023, June 28). History of the Maumee Watershed. ArcGIS StoryMaps. https://storym aps.arcgis.com/stories/7747914e22554eff8c64ee0f9569a14d

Annual events – Grand Rapids, Ohio. (n.d.). https://grandra pidsohio.com/attractions/annual-events/

Canal Experience - Metroparks Toledo. (n.d.). Metroparks Toledo. https://metroparkstoledo.com/features-and-rentals/c anal-experience/

Dray, A. (2018b, February 2). The unique village in Ohio where time stands still. OnlyInYourState®. https://www.onlyi nyourstate.com/experiences/ohio/unique-village-time-stands- still-oh

GDPR support. (n.d.). https://www.daytondailynews.com/n ews/local/miami-and-erie-canal-navigating-across-ohio/clQr 8nDQSkIk7BJiAFhFsN/

GRAND RAPIDS APPLEBUTTER FEST. (n.d.). GRAND RAPIDS APPLEBUTTER FEST. https://www.applebutterfest.org/

Jfox. (2021, June 8). 17 Curious facts about the Miami & Erie Canal - Cincinnati Magazine. Cincinnati Magazine. https://www.cincinnatimagazine.com/article/17-curious-facts-about-the-miami-erie-canal/

MapQuest. (n.d.). Antiques on Front, 24187 Front St, Grand Rapids, OH 43522, US - MapQuest. https://www.mapquest.com/us/ohio/antiques-on-front-275977787

morrowcountysentinel. (2016, July 26). Mount Gilead: A 19th century history of the village - Morrow County Sentinel. Morrow County Sentinel. https://www.morrowcountysentinel.com/2016/07/26/mount-gilead-a-19th-century-history-of-the-village/

Ohio Rhineland - Wikiwand. (n.d.). https://www.wikiwand.com/en/articles/Miami_and_Erie_Canal

Rhythm on the River: Bliss performs June 23. (2024, May 31). River Rat Country. https://riverratcountry.com/?p=470

The Fry site. (n.d.). Google Books. https://books.google.com/books/about/The_Fry_Site.html?id=jFB8y6XD7noC

Wikipedia contributors. (2024a, October 19). Grand Rapids, Ohio. Wikipedia. https://en.wikipedia.org/wiki/Grand_Rapids%2C_Ohio

Wikipedia contributors. (2024, November 20). Maumee River. Wikipedia. https://en.wikipedia.org/wiki/Maumee_River